Welcome ...

T0123823

You deserve complete happiness. No matter your age, faith, and financial or relationship status, happiness is just a matter of making some simple but effective changes to your attitude, perspective, and lifestyle. This book contains 60 powerful actions that you can read in just 30 seconds. The front of each page instructs you to do a simple exercise, and the back side offers insightful information on why that action will help you love life and be happy. Set this book in a visible place. Choose one action to do each day. The value and wisdom in each action will help you be truly happy and enjoy life to the fullest!

"*You must live in the present,
launch yourself on every wave,
find your eternity in each moment.
Fools stand on their island of opportunities
and look toward another land.*

*There is no other land;
there is no other life but this.*"

~ Henry David Thoreau

Enjoy Life and Be Happy
in 30 Seconds

By Alex A. Lluch
AUTHOR OF OVER 3 MILLION BOOKS SOLD

WS Publishing Group
San Diego, California

Enjoy Life and Be Happy in 30 Seconds

By Alex A. Lluch

Published by WS Publishing Group
San Diego, California 92119
Copyright © 2009 by WS Publishing Group

Designed by WS Publishing Group:
David Defenbaugh

For Inquiries:
Log on to www.WSPublishingGroup.com
E-mail info@WSPublishingGroup.com

ISBN 13: 978-1-934386-41-5

Printed in China

TODAY I WILL...

Focus on 5 things
that are great
in my life.

An old Swedish proverb states, "Worry often gives a small thing a big shadow." Indeed, we make mountains out of molehills by needlessly obsessing over things that are imperfect in our lives. Resist the urge to fixate on what you want to change about yourself or your circumstances. Instead, focus on 5 things that are great in your life, and channel your energy into those areas. Maybe you have a wonderful husband or a supportive circle of friends. Or perhaps you are great at tennis or are excelling in your guitar lessons. Focusing on the positive aspects of your life is the single most important step toward achieving true happiness.

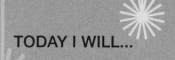

TODAY I WILL...

Use visualization techniques to improve my outlook.

Rhonda Byrne's book *The Secret* became an international bestseller nearly overnight. But the book's main premise is no secret at all. According to *The Secret*, the key to happiness and success is to picture yourself as a happy and successful person. Use visualization techniques to achieve this. For example, if you are trying to slim down, visualize yourself at your ideal weight. See yourself being active — exercising, dancing, or walking, for instance. See yourself at the beach wearing a new swimsuit. Feel the confidence you have. Create a new reality! This and other visualization techniques can help you build a positive outlook.

TODAY I WILL...

Forgive someone who
has hurt me.

Holding on to resentment is extremely unhealthy and can cause chronic health and emotional problems. Lighten your load by contacting someone you need to forgive and letting the person know that he or she has been forgiven. It is best to meet in person and speak face-to-face. If this is not possible, call this person on the phone or send a handwritten letter. Forgiving does not mean that you must forget the event. It simply means you set yourself free from negativity, bitterness, and anger. Feeling free through forgiveness is one of the many keys to being a more joyful person.

Make a heartfelt apology to someone I have wronged.

When someone tells you that you've hurt their feelings, listen intently. Fight the urge to become defensive. Don't get bogged down in the details of the event. Instead, focus on what you did or said that was hurtful. Take responsibility for your words and actions, be humble, and apologize. A heartfelt apology can go a long way in healing a wounded relationship. Apologizing when appropriate will also free you from guilt and shame, which are major obstacles to happiness. Through this process, you will obtain personal growth, strength of character, and the respect of others. The joy and peace of mind that you give to the other person when you make a heartfelt apology will be uplifting to you, as well.

TODAY I WILL...

Smile — even when I
don't feel like it.

Even if you don't feel like it, smile. It can make you feel better. Smiling releases endorphins, natural pain killers produced by the brain. In addition, put positive thinking behind your smile; a recent study by the Wake Forest University Baptist Medical Center found that thinking positively actually helps people overcome pain! In fact, Dr. Tetsuo Koyama, the lead author of the study, said, "Positive expectations produced about a 28 percent decrease in pain ratings — equal to a shot of morphine." So smile — it is a simple way to change the way you feel from the outside in.

TODAY I WILL...

Start a weekly
Gratitude Journal.

We all have positive experiences every day, but many of us concentrate on the negative ones. Daily gratitude will help you live life to the fullest. Start a Gratitude Journal and each week, make a list of your positive experiences and happy moments. Whether a stranger complimented your shoes or you tried a new restaurant you liked, no enjoyment is too small to write down. At the end of the week, notice how many little joys life presented in just a matter of days. As the saying goes, "Gratitude is the least of virtues; ingratitude the worst of vices." You will find that appreciating the small things you have to be grateful for will pave the way for bigger triumphs.

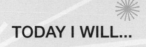

TODAY I WILL...

Look in the mirror and find 3 things I love about myself.

According to Planet Project, a global Internet polling company that polled 380,000 people in more than 225 countries, just 35 percent of all people enjoy the view when they look in the mirror. That means when 65 percent of the world's population looks in the mirror, they are disappointed! Improve your outlook by enjoying what you see. Look in the mirror each morning and find 3 things about yourself that you love. Say, "I have lovely eyes," "I like the way my hair looks today," or "My teeth are very white." After a while, you will learn to love the whole image.

Celebrate other people's successes to make way for my own windfalls.

Even though you may have a lot to be grateful for in your life, it is not uncommon to feel a twinge of jealousy or even bitterness when others experience success or triumph. Practice being the first to congratulate a friend, even if he or she receives something you wanted for yourself. If a friend calls to say she is engaged, instead of asking internally, "Why didn't this happen to me?" say out loud, "I'm so happy for you!" This is the best way to take power away from ugly feelings of jealousy or insecurity. Being a supportive friend paves the way for your own windfalls. Author Melody Beattie has said, "[Gratitude] can turn a meal into a feast, a house into a home, a stranger into a friend."

Pack a bag so
I am always ready for
an adventure.

Spontaneity is simply expressing a joy for life, so be open to all opportunities that arise. Truly, enjoying life requires creativity and a willingness to discover the opportunities for adventure that are all around us. If you see a festival, fair, or parade is happening in your neighborhood, drop everything and just go. Should you drive by a beautiful beach, stop and stick your feet in the sand. Make sure you will be ready for an adventure at a moment's notice by packing a bag that you keep in your car or at work. Pack things like sneakers, sunscreen, water, a swimsuit, and a jacket. Strive to be the kind of person who is always willing to go on a small adventure at the spur of the moment.

TODAY I WILL...

Thank my parents for everything they have done for me.

Raising children is never easy — a fact that we may not fully understand until we have our own families. Children definitely do not come with an instruction manual. However, despite the many challenges your parents probably faced, odds are, they did the best job they could raising you. There is much to thank them for — everything from ballet lessons to financial help to offering their unconditional love and support. No matter who you are, there are things you can admire and respect about your parents, so call them and thank them for being there for you over the years. Expressing your gratitude is both a way to show your appreciation and to acknowledge what a tough job being a parent is. You will find it quite uplifting to thank them for all they have done.

TODAY I WILL...

Volunteer to give back to my community.

Anne Frank wrote in her famous diary, "How wonderful it is that nobody need wait a single moment before starting to improve the world." Truly, enjoying life and being happy means contributing positively to your community. Giving your time to a worthy cause also helps put your own problems in perspective, gives you a sense of belonging within a community, and enhances your sense of self-worth. Research ways you can help, such as volunteering at a homeless shelter, writing letters to soldiers, picking up trash around your neighborhood, or helping out at the Humane Society. Serving your community will remind you that you have a purpose larger than yourself and helps you feel grateful for everything you have.

TODAY I WILL...

Commit a Random Act of Kindness.

The concept of Random Acts of Kindness gained popularity in the 1990s, even sparking a foundation by the same name. The idea is that with either planned or spontaneous acts of kindness, either toward friends or strangers, people can effect positive change in their communities as well as inspire others to pass kindness on. Random Acts of Kindness need not be spontaneous, though you should leave yourself open to the possibility of doing something kind for others at any moment. You might compliment a stranger, help someone with a flat tire, or offer to assist a neighbor with a home-improvement project. Committing Random Acts of Kindness will help you feel energized, positive, and uplifted.

Pick a room in my house and organize it.

Choose your bedroom, the garage, the kitchen, or any other room in your house and organize it to give you a sense of order and satisfaction. You will most likely discover you have more stuff than you have room for, so create boxes of clothes, toys, furniture, and housewares, and donate them to a homeless shelter or thrift store. After you have removed some of the clutter in the room, find a place for everything. Hang jackets on hooks or mount tools on a wall-rack, for instance. Once your giveaways have a new home and the room is arranged in an organized fashion, you will feel much more relaxed and happy. Now you can enjoy this room to the fullest!

Frame my favorite photos and hang them around my house.

Decorate your living space with things that mean something to you. Frame favorite photographs of friends and family so your home is infused with their presence. Hang pictures on the walls or place them on your nightstand so you can revisit them frequently. Prominently display diplomas, certificates, or other markers of success that make you proud. Also, whenever you travel, pick up a piece that can be displayed somewhere that will remind you of your adventure. When you are surrounded by this memorabilia, you will be reminded of all the fun you've had with the great people you know. Filling your home with warm memories makes it a space in which you want to spend your time.

TODAY I WILL...

Use my influence to help someone else.

There are many ways to use your influence to help others. Pass a qualified friend's résumé along to your boss. Did you witness an accident or a crime? Notify the police and tell them what you saw. If you notice a person taking advantage of someone less capable, step in and help. For instance, if you notice that a merchant is overcharging an elderly person, point out the actual price and help with the transaction. Appropriately intervening on behalf of others will make you feel capable and important.

Show appreciation for a special person in my life.

Most people remember special days such as birthdays and anniversaries. But you should also select other occasions to show people how much they mean to you. This will greatly enhance your relationships. When shopping, pick up an extra treat for your mother. Plan an unexpected movie night for you and a good friend. Bring home dinner from your wife's favorite restaurant to show her how much you care. What you do to express your appreciation is not as important as the thought behind it. Unexpected, thoughtful acts will inject new energy into your relationships and happiness in your life.

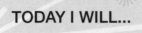

TODON I WILL...

Get a great
night's sleep.

Getting 8 hours of sleep every night is important to your overall well-being. Studies show that lack of sleep heightens the risk for cancer, heart disease, and diabetes. Additionally, not getting enough sleep leads to stress and overeating. In fact, research has shown adults who sleep less than 7 hours a night are significantly more likely to be obese. Some tips for getting a great night's sleep include reading to relax before bed; writing down a list of things that are on your mind, then trusting yourself to deal with them the next day; making your bedroom a sanctuary, meaning no TV, no work, and no bills in the room; and sticking to a regular sleep schedule, even on the weekends. Getting a good night's sleep will help you enjoy each day to the fullest.

Eat smaller meals
more often to have
more energy!

For energy-filled, positive days, eat 6 small meals instead of 3 large ones. Eating smaller, more frequent meals will increase your metabolism and keep insulin levels even throughout the entire day. Waiting too long between meals teaches your body to "save up" fat and shift into starvation mode to conserve energy. This can slow your metabolism and make you feel lethargic. Eat small meals about every 3 hours to maintain energy levels throughout the day.

Limit caffeine and sugar intake.

According to Johns Hopkins University School of Medicine, 80 to 90 percent of North American adults and more than 165 million Americans report using caffeine regularly. In fact, caffeine is the world's most commonly used drug. However, caffeine and sugar can also lead to rapid heart rate, feelings of anxiety and irritability, and increased fatigue after the effects wear off. Instead, give yourself a natural boost by eating a light, healthy snack such as yogurt, nuts, or fruit. Re-up your energy by taking a brisk walk or stretching. There are many ways to reenergize without the harmful and negative after-effects of overindulging in caffeine and sugar. Avoid heavy intake to keep you energized and focused.

TODAY I WILL...

Meditate to relieve stress.

Meditation can be a wonderful stress-relieving exercise. It can be done easily, quickly, inexpensively, and almost anywhere. Meditation instantly calms you by increasing blood flow and slowing the heart rate. Just 5 minutes of it can have powerful healing and restorative effects. According to the National Institutes of Health, "Meditation techniques offer the potential of learning how to live in an increasingly complex and stressful society while helping to preserve health in the process." So find a quiet spot, sit comfortably, and imagine a peaceful place. Take slow, deep breaths. Clear your mind of all stressors. In no time, meditation may become your favorite way to relax!

* * * * * * * * * * *

TODAY I WILL...

Limit my alcohol intake.

Enjoy a glass of wine with dinner or an ice-cold beer at a summer barbecue — but don't overdo it. Remember, alcohol impairs your ability to think and function. Alcohol also prevents your liver from breaking down sugar, which turns into stored fat and leads to a "beer belly" or "wine tire." Although a second glass of wine may feel good at the time, the next day you may feel sluggish or hungover, which will cause you to be unprepared for work and other activities. Remember, alcohol is a depressant, so use it sparingly. Find fun social events that don't include alcohol — you'll feel better day to day.

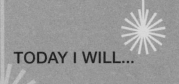

TODAY I WILL...

Exercise to give my
body a natural high.

Be sure to get at least 30 minutes of physical activity every day. Many of us think we are too busy to exercise, but you should always make exercise a priority in your schedule. Try using half of your lunch break to go for a brisk walk. Or, go for a jog around your neighborhood before or after dinner. When you exercise, your body releases endorphins, which naturally elevate your mood and give you more energy to get through your day. In addition, when you get fit you will look fantastic, feel great about your body, and have less risk for illness. Take advantage of all the benefits of exercise every day to enjoy life to the fullest.

TODAY I WILL...

Drink 8 glasses of
water to stay hydrated.

Water does more than quench your thirst; it is the most important element in the human body! Water is essential to all your bodily functions — including brain function, digesting food, and producing blood. Your body is made up of more than 50 percent water, so, to replenish it, you must drink 8 glasses of water daily — more if you exercise or play sports. Staying hydrated flushes harmful toxins out of your body, gives you more energy, and boosts your metabolism. Also, hydration will give you soft skin and better skin elasticity (no wrinkles!). When you look and feel great, you can better enjoy life, so stay hydrated for your health and happiness.

TODAY I WILL...

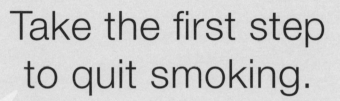
Take the first step
to quit smoking.

The frightening truth is, about half of all 45 million U.S. smokers who continue will end up dying from a smoking-related illness. Quitting smoking will greatly reduce your risk for developing respiratory ailments, heart disease, and smoking-related cancers. Amazingly, your body begins to heal just 20 minutes after your last cigarette! Former smokers consistently testify that they are much happier than when they smoked. Start by assessing your habit, then think of ways to taper off, as well as healthy options for replacing cigarettes in your day. By taking the first step toward quitting smoking, you will instantly be healthier and better able to enjoy life. Visit cdc.gov/tobacco for tips on quitting.

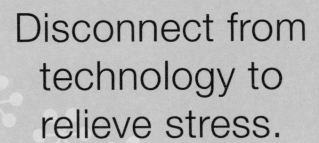

TODAY I WILL...

Disconnect from technology to relieve stress.

Part of the reason stress is such a widespread problem is that everyone is constantly "plugged in." People spend their waking hours tied to email, cell phones, computers, and other instruments that keep them connected while on the go. Some people even sleep with their cell phones! If this is your lifestyle, be sure to make time to unplug. Turn off your phone and computer for at least 1 hour a day while you are not working. Shut off your cell phone while you sleep. You will be much more relaxed and peaceful without being interrupted.

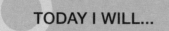

TODAY I WILL...

Reach out to a friend in need.

Think about your friends, neighbors, and coworkers — is there someone who may need your help right now? Reach out to this person, and think of what you can do to help their situation. You might cook dinner for a friend with a new baby. Or, if you know a coworker is going through a breakup, invite him or her to join you for lunch one afternoon. Reaching out could be as simple as stopping by to chat with an elderly neighbor who doesn't get many visitors. You just might be the bright spot in someone's otherwise dark or difficult day, which can really make you feel wonderful.

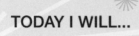

TODAY I WILL...

Honor a loved one
I have lost.

Losing a loved one is devastating, and grief can be a long process. However, remembering a loved one does not have to be sad or depressing; you can rejoice in happy memories of friends and family who have passed by honoring them in your daily life. When you are missing your mother, eat at her favorite restaurant or make a recipe she loved. If a friend has passed away, make a donation to her favorite charity in her name. Or, if your grandfather enjoyed fishing, take a fishing trip and think of him fondly. When you honor a lost loved one, you feel close to him or her, and take a wonderful step toward happiness and joy.

TODAY I WILL...

Make a date with myself.

Make a date with yourself! When you make time for yourself, you relieve the stress in your life, thus making you a better coworker, friend, and family member. So block out some time just for you and honor that commitment. If something comes up, treat the time you have planned with yourself as any other appointment, and keep it. See a movie, enjoy a homemade dinner and a glass of wine, or stay in and take a hot bath. Nurturing the relationship you have with yourself brings daily joy and is the model for the happy relationships you have with others.

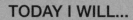

TODAY I WILL...

Stop sweating
the small stuff.

The line at the bank may be 20 people long. Your spouse may forget to pick up your clothes from the dry cleaner. A friend may flake on lunch plans at the last moment. Traffic might be a nightmare. It is tempting to get upset, but, more often than not, these things are small things that are easy to let go. Not sweating the small stuff means evaluating how important a grievance is to you and assessing how willing you are to get angry or engage in an argument over it. Picking your battles wisely will keep you from feeling stressed out over petty things. Instead, read a magazine while waiting in line at the bank. Find a good song on the radio during a traffic jam. When you stop sweating the small stuff, every day will be a breeze.

Make a scrapbook or photo album to document my life.

To fully enjoy life, we must appreciate the lives of those who have gone before us, paved the way for us, and made us who we are. You and your ancestors have a special story that makes you *you*. In this spirit, make a scrapbook or album that documents your life and your family's life. Draw a family tree, tell the story of your history and countries of origin, and share pictures of loved ones. Make scrapbooks of you and your friends' adventures. Documenting your life will bring back a flood of amazing, happy memories and inspire you to make new ones.

✶ ✶ ✶ ✶ ✶ ✶ ✶ ✶ ✶ ✶

TODAY I WILL...

Make a master list and divide household responsibilities.

Household chores can be a real pain if not everyone is doing their share. Make a master list of all the tasks that keep your household running smoothly, such as cooking, cleaning, transportation, childcare, maintenance, and bill paying. Make a spreadsheet with categories for daily, weekly, monthly, and bimonthly chores, then divide the list among your family members or roommates. Hang the spreadsheet in a place where everyone can see it, such as in the kitchen. Hold household members accountable to completing their chores. If you have young children, provide some incentive by planning fun activities, outings, or even prizes for those who complete their chores on time. Eliminating conflict over household chores will make life at your house much happier.

TODAY I WILL...

Create and stick to a budget.

In the 21st century, the majority of American couples are living beyond their means. A recent study showed that, in just one year, Americans charged $2.2 trillion in purchases and cash advances on major credit cards. Living beyond your means creates stress and worry and threatens the security of your family. Make a budget that tracks both essential and discretionary expenses. A budget should include items such as household bills, credit obligations, incidentals, discretionary funds, hidden costs, emergency funds, and money for savings or vacations. Creating a budget allows you to evaluate your current spending and make cutbacks or expansions in necessary areas. Sticking to it will keep you happy and worry-free.

TODAY I WILL...

Say "No" if I am
in over my head.

Having too many obligations is sure to stress anyone out. Therefore, it is important to say no to nonessential social events. Though it is nice to be invited to parties, it is not necessary to accept every invitation. Similarly, if a friend asks a favor of you, and you simply don't have the time, apologize, and decline. Saying "No" will not only reduce stress but also keep you healthy. According to the Centers for Disease Control, the leading 6 causes of death in the U.S. — heart disease, cancer, lung ailments, accidents, cirrhosis of the liver, and suicide — are all brought on at least in part by stress. Feel empowered to say "No" when it is appropriate and in your best interest. Love yourself enough to set limits on what can be demanded of you.

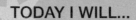

TODAY I WILL...

Create a list of
things I want to do
in my lifetime.

One way to plan to enjoy life to the fullest is to create a list of things you want to do in your lifetime. Some will be simple, such as "try a new cuisine" or "camp out under the stars." Others may call for some planning, such as "plant a garden," "get to know my neighbors," or "build a wine collection." Still other things on your list will require lots of foresight and preparation, such as "hike through a rainforest," "visit the Great Wall of China," or "learn to scuba dive." Don't limit yourself, as you have your entire life to complete everything on your list. The wonderful part of this exercise is you get to dream — either alone, with friends, or with your spouse — and plan for future adventures.

TODAY I WILL...

Laugh out loud often.

Studies show that laughter reduces stress, lowers blood pressure, elevates mood, and boosts the immune system. Laughter also improves brain functioning, increases oxygen in the blood, fosters connection with others, and makes you feel good all over. Children in nursery school laugh approximately 300 times a day, while adults laugh, at most, only 17 times per day. So why should children reap all the benefits? See a funny movie, read a daily joke, or just share a laugh with friends. Incorporate a good chuckle into your day to reduce stress and promote relaxation and happiness.

Expand my social circle by making one new friend.

To increase happiness and extend your life, incorporate new and interesting people into your social circle. A recent study published in the *Journal of Epidemiology and Community Health* found that having a network of good friends can extend a person's lifespan. Another study linked positive, nurturing friendships with healthier exercise, diet, and sleeping habits. Gravitate toward friends with similar values, goals, and interests and who share your positive attitude about life. Meet new people while doing the things you love, be that playing a sport, shopping, or attending a book club. All your friends should give you a sense of support and belonging. Invigorating friendships will benefit your health, attitude, emotional well-being, and inner peace.

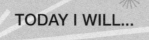

TODAY I WILL...

Turn off the TV and
do a hands-on activity.

Openness, flexibility, and creativity are keys to a healthy social life. Start by turning off the television; watching a sitcom or movie can be relaxing, but it won't help you enjoy life to the fullest. Instead of sedentary activities like watching TV, choose hands-on activities that will expand your cultural horizons or help you find new creative interests. Consider volunteering, taking cooking classes, joining a political organization, attending wine-tasting events, getting a membership at a museum, joining an improv comedy group, signing up for art classes — even karaoke counts as a creative endeavor. Your life will be fuller and happier when you meet new people who you can participate in fun, hands-on activities.

Make my bedroom a sanctuary for relaxation.

Your bedroom is a place for rest, relaxation, and intimacy, so treat it as such. Decorate your room using cool, relaxing colors such as blues, purples, and greens. Hang pictures of whatever relaxes you or reminds you of happy times — pictures from your wedding day, a favorite trip, images of family and friends, or vistas of natural beauty. Clear out clutter and remove unnecessary distractions. Watch TV in another room. Keep items that heighten your stress levels — such as bills, work, or medical items — in a separate corner of the house that you visit infrequently. Invest in luxurious sheets and a soft comforter. Buy a small CD player and listen to relaxing music. When your bedroom is a sanctuary, you will sleep better and wake up feeling revived.

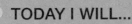
TODAY I WILL...

Treat myself to a massage.

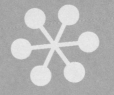

Treat yourself to relaxing indulgences such as a massage. Massage therapy helps to relieve tension headaches, eye strain, muscle tension, and stiffness. A massage can cost between $55 and $125, but how many times have we spent more than that in a store and still come home feeling sad or lonely? Massages do not have to be expensive. Many massage schools offer discounted services so that their students can practice their skills. Or, ask a friend or partner to exchange massages. If massages are not your thing, try indulging in another relaxing activity to reduce stress, such as a daytime nap or a long, hot bath.

TODAY I WILL...

Organize a food drive.

Heartbreakingly, the National Coalition for the Homeless estimates there are as many as 3.5 million homeless in the U.S., 39 percent of whom are children. Surveys also showed that 40 percent of these people go at least 1 day a month with nothing to eat. You can help those less fortunate than you by creating a food drive. This can be simple — just have friends and coworkers spread the word, then set out boxes in your store or office. Collect canned and dry goods and drop them off at a local charitable organization or shelter when you have reached your goal. Helping others will give you a sense of accomplishment, as well as appreciation for the good in your own life.

✶ ✶ ✶ ✶ ✶ ✶ ✶ ✶ ✶ ✶

Find a hobby
that relaxes me
and indulge in it.

Make time each week for a hobby that you find relaxing. For instance, take a pottery or painting class — you will likely find it satisfying to produce something beautiful with your own hands that you can be proud of. Or, you might take up a physical hobby, such as fly-fishing or tennis. It will feel great to do something active and be in the fresh air. Hobbies have been medically proven to reduce stress and increase happiness. In one study, published in the *Journal of the American Medical Association,* female heart patients reported significant decreases in heart rate and blood pressure while working on a simple craft project. Improved health is just one example of the many positive benefits a hobby will bring to your life.

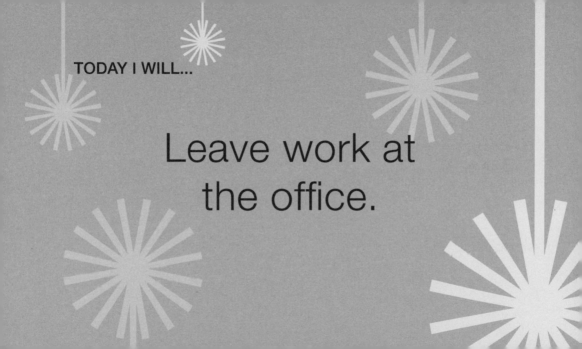

TODAY I WILL...

Leave work at the office.

Writer Margaret Fuller once noted, "Men for the sake of getting a living forget to live." If you find yourself devoting inordinate chunks of time to work, or bringing stress from work home with you, ask yourself how it is affecting your relationships. You are probably neglecting friends, pets, and family — or yourself! The world is not likely to fall apart if you do not return a phone call immediately, so it makes no sense to add such stress to your life. Refrain from working more than 9 hours a day, and take at least 1 day a week to not work at all. Instead of working yourself to the point of exhaustion every day, make sure the hours you spend at work are quality ones. Then, spend your time off with the people you love.

TODAY I WILL...

Plan a getaway!

According to a study by the travel company Expedia, American workers collectively give back 175 million paid vacation days to their employers every year. You work hard — so use your vacation days! Getting away doesn't have to take lots of money or time — a night spent in a local bed and breakfast, or a weekend devoted to exploring a nearby destination can be just as significant as an exotic beach vacation. Better still, an escape can reignite your love life! Taking a vacation is a perfect way to inspire romance and reconnect with a loved one. A change of scenery is always rejuvenating, so plan an escape today. The important thing is to get away and enjoy a little time off.

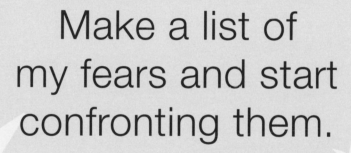

Make a list of
my fears and start
confronting them.

Writer Henry S. Haskins thought of fear in the following way: "Panic at the thought of doing a thing is a challenge to do it." Make a list of your greatest fears, then turn them on their heads by confronting them. If you feel crowded in public places (as do 1 in 5 Americans, according to the National Institute of Mental Health), purposely seek out a crowd and become part of it. If you fear the dentist (as do 58 percent of Americans), schedule an appointment with your dentist to have him or her explain what goes on during a check-up and cleaning. Confronting your fears will demystify them, allowing them to be conquered.

TODAY I WILL...

Record my accomplishments to silence my inner critic.

The first step to becoming immune to the criticisms of others is to silence the critic within yourself. As an African proverb states, "When there is no enemy within, the enemies outside cannot hurt you." Counteract nasty self-talk with reassuring, productive thoughts. Keep a running tally of your accomplishments to banish self-criticism — everything from praise you received at work to a delicious new dinner you cooked. Even the seemingly small things are relevant, and what you make of your accomplishments is what matters. For instance, if you try ice skating, you can be happy that you were able to go around the rink twice, or you can be unhappy because you were *only* able to go around the rink twice. The choice is yours.

TODAY I WILL...

Change my daily routine.

Often, we struggle with boredom and unhappiness because we have fallen into a rut. People often carry out their daily routine without a thought. Stop sleepwalking through your day! Change your daily routine, and you will reinvigorate your life. This can be as simple as driving a new route to work, trying an exotic food, or rock climbing instead of working out at the gym. Mixing up your routine is a great start toward challenging yourself, building confidence, breaking out of a rut, and discovering new adventures. You will be amazed at how reenergized you feel after making even a small change to your daily routine.

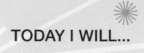

TODAY I WILL...

Incorporate Feng Shui
in my home.

The ancient practice of Feng Shui says that the choices you make when decorating affect your quality of life. Remove the clutter in your home, which blocks the flow of positive energy, or chi. Observe these rules of Feng Shui when cleaning out and rearranging your home: Avoid dark colors and heavy curtains that may weigh you down and anchor your mood; use mirrors to make rooms look larger, but never directly across from your bed; place flowering plants in groups of 3 near the entrance to your home; don't have a television in your bedroom; and don't leave shoes by the front door. Feng Shui opens your personal space to allow positive energy to move freely.

Rediscover my city.

Do you want a new, fun way to reconnect with friends or just get reenergized? Pretend to be a tourist in your own town. Go online and download a list of the 50 top things to see and do in your city. Or, buy a guidebook, check the entertainment section of your local newspaper, or head out to a restaurant or play that was reviewed on the radio. Take a bike tour, see a concert, visit a museum, or check out a local landmark. Take pictures and buy souvenirs. You will feel reinvigorated by your city and your time spent with friends exploring a fascinating place — your home! Rediscovering your city will get you excited about where you live and help you find new activities in your city.

TODAY I WILL...

Join a gym.

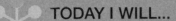

Joining a gym can greatly contribute to a happier, healthier life. Not only are you able to work out and get in shape, but you are surrounded by countless opportunities to meet new people. When you become more active you are likely to make friends who share your interest in exercise and fitness. This can help keep you motivated to exercise, and, with your newfound self-confidence, you are also more likely to strike up a conversation and pursue new opportunities for socializing. This will result in an improvement in your overall quality of life. There are many kinds of gyms, offering a variety of amenities, classes, and programs. Find one that is right for you, and enjoy the health and social benefits.

Personalize my workspace.

You will be able to do better work if your workspace is clean, organized, and feels more personal. While you don't want to clutter your desk, your day will be brighter if you customize your workspace with items that show your personality. Put up a few photos of your friends and family. Hang a calendar that shows one of your interests, like dogs or beautiful beaches. Bring in a special coffee mug from home. Or, use a colorful cup as a pencil holder. Your personalized workspace will make you smile and may even invite friendly inquiries from coworkers. Even if you work from home, you can keep your desk personal and inspiring.

* * * * * * * * * *

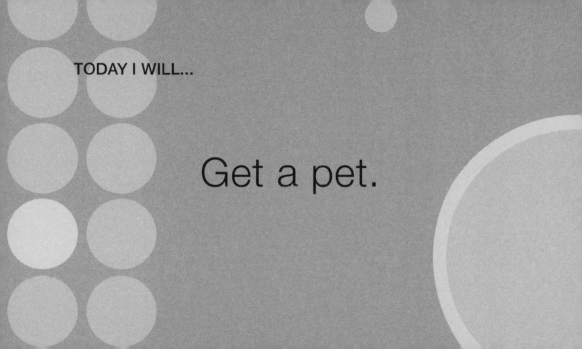

Studies have shown that people who have regular interaction with pets are happier and healthier. The Centers for Disease Control reports that having pets can lower your blood pressure, cholesterol, and reduce feelings of loneliness by increasing opportunities for exercise, outdoor activities, and socialization. Just try not to smile when you are greeted by a loving pet whose entire life revolves around you, even after fighting traffic for an hour. A recent study showed that stockbrokers in New York who had dogs or cats as pets had lower blood pressure than those who did not. Finally, adding a pet to your home ensures that you will always have company. Get a dog, cat, fish, bird, or other pet to further enjoy life.

Eliminate one thing
in my life that
brings me down.

To be truly happy, sometimes you must eliminate unhealthy people and situations from your life. For instance, you might feel stuck in a dead-end job. Resolve to take the first step toward finding a new one. Or, perhaps there is a person in your life who constantly brings you down. Interestingly, a recent survey showed that almost half (48 percent) of women admitted to having a toxic friend who has prevented them from spending time with the people they truly care about. If there is someone or something in your life that isn't making you happy, stop wasting your time! It may take some courage to eliminate this stuff from your life, but you will feel much more fulfilled once you are able to concentrate on the people and things that do make you happy.

Dance to my favorite song.

Mayo Clinic researchers have concluded that dancing reduces stress, increases energy, improves strength, and increases coordination. Grab a few minutes in the evening to dance to your favorite song. Taking time to move your body when no one is watching frees you from feeling self-conscious. Spending time celebrating your body through movement improves self-esteem and is great exercise.

TODAY I WILL...

Try a new recipe.

Cooking can be a relaxing way to wind down at the end of the day. Cooking for your significant other, or even just for yourself, can be interesting and fun if you constantly try out new recipes. If you're cooking for one, prepare tasty dishes that can be broken down into single servings and frozen. Most of all, make dining a pleasant experience. Use a nice placemat and a cloth napkin. Sip a glass of wine or sparkling water with dinner. Set a relaxing mood by lighting candles and playing music. Savor each bite and take your time. Enjoy your meal and your great company.

Act like a kid again.

As children, we were all more open to the moment, delighted by new things, and less self-conscious. We were quick to laugh and play alongside anyone and explore uncharted territory without hesitance. To revisit the wonder of a child's carefree lifestyle, spend some time acting like a kid again. Be playful at home: Put on music and dance around, dust off that Frisbee, or play a board game. Visit the zoo or an amusement park. Fingerpaint. The key is to do something silly and fun and not to take life too seriously. Acting like a kid again, no matter your age, is a great way to enjoy life without stress or fear.

TODAY I WILL...

Write a list of regrets, then throw it away.

How often have you lamented, "If only I had done that," or "If only that had happened to me"? Author Mercedes Lackay has written, "If only. Those must be the two saddest words in the world." Indeed, regret is possibly the most useless emotion, because it holds us prisoner to what cannot be undone. Let go of these feelings by writing a list of everything you regret in your life. Then, take the paper and crumple it into a ball or tear it to shreds. Throw the paper away. This physical act symbolizes eliminating remorse and regret from your life. The best you can do is take a lesson from each situation, then see the future with a happy, positive outlook.

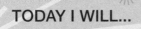
TODAY I WILL...

Create a list of goals
for the coming month.

To jumpstart a newfound feeling of accomplishment, create a list of goals for the next 30 days. These should be things you can complete on a daily or weekly basis, such as getting your oil changed, reading a good book, or cleaning out the garage. Hang your list in a highly visible place. Reviewing this list often will remind you of the things that are important to you. In turn, this will make you work on the steps that will help you achieve these goals. Cross items off your list as you do them. This will give you an immediate sense of satisfaction and keep you motivated toward the next item on your list.

TODAY I WILL...

Break large jobs into small, manageable tasks.

At times it is hard to stay confident when a giant task is looming over you. Before beginning, break the job down into smaller, more manageable parts. If every corner of your house is an unsightly mess, deal with each room one at a time. If you have been asked to make Thanksgiving dinner, break the meal up and tackle the dishes one by one. Always acknowledge when you have accomplished a task by crossing it off a larger list. Tackling smaller components of a larger goal will keep you feeling motivated, which positively impacts your overall outlook and chances of success.

Stop relying on other people for my happiness.

Never enter into a relationship thinking it is going to become the sole source of your happiness. You are not one-half of a person, looking for another half to complete you. You are responsible for your own happiness. As the adage goes, you cannot be truly loved by another person until you find peace and joy within yourself. Your happiness is simply not something that others can provide. Relationships should enhance your joy, not serve as its sole source. Nurture the relationship you have with yourself and you'll never have to rely on anyone else for your happiness.

TODAY I WILL...

Enjoy life
and be happy.

Actress Mae West once said, "You only live once, but if you do it right, once is enough." She was correct in that life is an ongoing process of changing, discovering, making mistakes, and moving forward. Being truly happy is the culmination of many other states of being, such as feeling peace, pleasure, satisfaction, and joy. Enjoying life includes walking around with a smile on your face, savoring the day you just had, and also looking forward to tomorrow. Remember that no decision you make is final. Every dream can be pursued. Commit yourself to your happiness. Nurture your relationships with others, and with yourself. By taking the obstacles you encounter as opportunities to learn, help others, and better yourself, you can and will lead a happier, more fulfilling life.